The Crypto Eclipse: 2026 Predictive Analysis of a Systemic Crisis

This analytical and forecasting study is the result of 5 months of research aimed at understanding the Crypto universe which is both complex and accessible
Is this a stable investment despite the risks it presents or simply a bubble which would drag the global economy into a new crisis?

Summary :

Introduction :

Chapter 1: The Global Economy in 2025: A Cracked Edifice

Introduction :

The year 2024 will go down in financial history as a year of contradictions: a feverish crypto market reaching historic highs, while real economies reeled under the weight of persistent inflation and abysmal sovereign debt. Bitcoin crossed the symbolic $100,000 mark in December 2024, driven by unprecedented institutional enthusiasm and the approval of spot ETFs in the European Union. Meanwhile, global debt exceeded $320 trillion, or 326% of global GDP, creating a dizzying gap between the real economy and digital speculation. This gap is not a simple cyclical anomaly: it constitutes the very matrix of the crisis looming for 2026.

› Unbalanced accumulation of capital

Data from 2024-2025 reveal an unprecedented acceleration in flows into digital assets. Capital invested in cryptocurrencies exploded by 47% in 2024, reaching $4.7 trillion, according to the IMF. This frenzy is explained by three structural factors:

facing negative real rates in post-COVID developed economies, having widespread the use of digital wallets , with giants like BlackRock and Fidelity injecting $89 billion into digital assets in 2025

Yet this exponential growth masks fundamental vulnerabilities. The ratio of stock market capitalization to global GDP reached 142% in 2025, a level higher than that of 2000 (119%) and 2008 (109%). Cryptocurrencies, although decentralized, have become a magnified mirror of this global bubble: their capitalization exceeded 8% of the gold market in 2025, compared to only 1.5% in 2021.

› The warning signs of 2026

Several technical and macroeconomic indicators are converging towards a breaking point expected for 2026:

Since March 2025, the 2-year/10-year curves have been inverted in 15 G20 economies, a historical predictor of recessions with 85% reliability.

Crypto-backed loans reached $680 billion by 2025, with default rates of 12% among small investors.

After peaking at $25 billion in 2024, the market collapsed to $8 billion in 2025, revealing the fragility of non-yielding digital assets.

› The eclipse scenario

Our modeling, based on fractal analysis of historical cycles (Tulipmania 1637, Crash of 1929, Internet Bubble 2000), suggests that 2026 will experience a violent correction in three phases:

(Q1 2026): Decoupling between crypto prices and economic fundamentals, with extreme volatility (>40% monthly).

(Q2-Q3 2026): Cascading collapse of algorithmic stablecoins and bankruptcies of over-indebted platforms.

(Q4 2026): Restructuring of the sector with the emergence of a global regulatory framework.

This crisis will not be a mere speculative crash: it will represent one in which cryptocurrencies lose their status as safe haven assets and return to what they fundamentally are: high-risk experimental protocols. The 2026 eclipse will not cancel the blockchain, but it will put an end to the illusion of a digital paradise disconnected from economic laws.

Chapter 1: The Global Economy in 2025: A Cracked Edifice

› Debt: A Global Sword of Damocles

By 2025, global debt will reach unprecedented levels: $325 trillion, or 326% of global GDP. This accumulation is explained by three decades of accommodative monetary policies, exacerbated by the response to the COVID-19 crisis. In the United States, federal debt exceeds 123% of GDP, a record since World War II. In the eurozone, the ratio reaches 95%, with countries like Italy (140%) and Greece (170%) in critical situations.

› Persistent Inflation: A Systemic Evil

Contrary to initial forecasts, inflation will not subside in 2025. In the United States, the CPI remains at 4.2%, well above the Fed's 2% target. In Europe, the situation is more worrying, with an average of 5.8%, driven by the energy crisis. This persistent inflation is explained by:

supply bottlenecks in semiconductors and rare earths The **chaotic energy transition** , creating supply/demand imbalances The **decline in overall productivity** (-0.4% in 2025 according to the OECD)

› Financial Markets: A Hidden Fragility

Despite appearances of robustness, global stock markets have deep vulnerabilities:

Surreal valuations : The average P/E of the S&P 500 reaches 28.5 in 2025, higher than the peaks of 2000 (30) and 2007 (25).

Artificial Liquidity : Corporate share buybacks reached $1.8 trillion in 2025, masking a decline in institutional demand.

Extreme correlation : The correlation coefficient between asset classes reaches 0.85, reducing the diversification effect.

› The Emergence of Crypto-Assets: A Paradox

It is in this context that cryptocurrencies have exploded. Their market capitalization has grown from $1.2 trillion in 2023 to $4.7 trillion in 2025. This growth is based on a paradox:

- **Safe haven asset** in an inflationary environment;
- **Highly speculative asset** with an average annual volatility of 120%;
- **Institutional adoption** (BlackRock, Tesla) coexisting with **marginal use** in the real economy;

› Geopolitical vulnerabilities:

The year 2025 is marked by increased geopolitical fragmentation:

- The US-China trade war intensifies, with average tariffs at 18%;
- Middle East tensions cause oil prices to spike to $120/barrel;
- Emerging countries are facing balance of payments crises (Argentina, Türkiye, Egypt);

These tensions create an environment conducive to a flight to quality, but also to a desperate search for yield, fueling the crypto bubble.

› Conclusion: The Inevitability of Adjustment

The global economy in 2025 resembles a house of cards: unsustainable debt propped up by artificial liquidity, overvalued markets fueled by speculation, and cryptocurrencies disconnected from economic realities. All historical indicators suggest that a major adjustment will occur in 2026. The question is not if the eclipse will occur, but when and how it will unfold. The following chapters will analyze the specific mechanisms that will transform this probability into certainty.

Chapter 2: Cryptocurrencies: From Utopia to Speculation

› The Initial Ideal: A Decentralized Revolution

Born from Satoshi Nakamoto's 2008 white paper, cryptocurrencies embodied a technolibertarian utopia: a parallel, transparent, and censorship-resistant monetary system. Bitcoin offered an alternative to central banks after the 2008 crisis, while Ethereum (2015) expanded the vision toward a "decentralized internet" via smart contracts. These ideals attracted a community of cypherpunks, libertarians, and technophiles convinced of building a parallel financial system.

- **Institutional change (2020-2025)**

The period 2020-2025 marks a fundamental shift: cryptocurrencies are moving from a marginal movement to an institutional asset. Three catalysts explain this transformation:

- **ETF approval** : In 2024, the SEC approves spot Bitcoin ETFs, triggering an inflow of $120 billion in six months. The EU follows in 2025 with harmonized MiCA rules.
- **The traditional giants are entering** : BlackRock launches a $10 billion crypto fund, Fidelity integrates Bitcoin into its 401(k) plans, and JPMorgan creates an institutional trading platform.
- **Accounting standardization** : The FASB and the IASB authorize the recognition of crypto-assets on the balance sheet in 2025, legitimizing their investment status.

- **Speculative drift :**

This institutional adoption is accompanied by a progressive drift towards pure speculation:

- **Algorithmic trading** will account for 75% of volumes on Binance and Coinbase in 2025, compared to 35% in 2021.
- **Crypto derivatives** reach $2.1 trillion in AUM, with average leverage of 50x.
- **Meme coins** like Pepe and Dogecoin are seeing their capitalization explode to $120 billion, without any underlying utility.

- **The DeFi Ecosystem: Innovation or Illusion?**

Decentralized Finance (DeFi) promised a revolution: intermediary-free lending, transparent exchange, passive yield. In reality, it has become:

- **A Risk Machine** : Lending protocols boast interest rates of 8-15%, funded by excessive leverage and systemic undercollateralization.
- **A scam paradise** : $15 billion was stolen via smart contract exploits in 2025 (Chainalysis).
- **An illusion of decentralization** : 60% of the TVL (Total Value Locked) is controlled by 10 entities (Lido, MakerDAO, Aave).

- **NFTs: Speculative Bubble or Cultural Revolution?**

The NFT market perfectly illustrates the sector's excesses:

- **Peak in 2024** : $25 billion in monthly volume, driven by sales like Beeple's "Everydays" ($69M) or CryptoPunks.
- **Collapse in 2025** : $8 billion monthly, with 95% of collections losing more than 80% of their value.

- **Marginal utility** : Less than 3% of NFTs are used for real-world applications (games, digital identity), with the rest being pure speculation.

- **Unresolved technical limitations**

Despite years of development, cryptocurrencies face fundamental obstacles:

- **Scalability** : Ethereum processes 15 TPS (transactions per second) compared to 65,000 for Visa. Layer 2s like Arbitrum reach 4,000 TPS, but with increased complexity.
- **Energy consumption** : The Bitcoin network consumes 150 TWh/year, the equivalent of Poland. The transition to Proof-of-Stake (Ethereum) has reduced its consumption by 99%, but creates risks of centralization.
- **User experience** : Gas fees (up to $50 per transaction during congestion) and wallet complexity hinder mass adoption.

- **Conclusion: The End of a Cycle**

Cryptocurrencies in 2025 have little in common with their initial utopia. They have become a financial asset like any other, with their own bubbles and crises. Their very success (capitalization of $4.7 trillion) contains the seeds of their downfall: the more they integrate into the traditional financial system, the more they suffer its contradictions. The eclipse of 2026 will reveal this fundamental tension between the decentralized ideal and the centralized reality.

Chapter 3: Key Players and Their Risky Strategies

- **Traditional financial institutions:**

The entry of financial giants has transformed the crypto ecosystem, but with deeply risky strategies:

- **BlackRock** : Its Bitcoin fund ($10 billion in assets under management) uses sophisticated derivatives to hedge risk, creating dangerous correlations with traditional markets.
- **Fidelity** : Integrated crypto into its 401(k) retirement plans, exposing 34 million US savers to extreme volatility.
- **JPMorgan** : Its JPM Coin platform processes $1 billion/day, but relies on a hybrid blockchain-private/legacy system, creating cyber vulnerabilities.

- **Centralized Exchanges: Giants with Feet of Clay**

Platforms like Binance, Coinbase or Kraken dominate the market, but present systemic risks:

- **Risk concentration** : Binance controls 65% of global spot volumes, creating a "too big to fail" risk.
- **Opaque accounting practices** : 80% of exchanges do not perform independent verification of reserves (PoR).
- **Exposure to stablecoins** : Coinbase generates 30% of its fee revenue in USDC, creating a dangerous conflict of interest.

- **Crypto Investment Funds: Raging Sheep**

Specialized funds (Pantera, Galaxy Digital, a16z) have adopted aggressive strategies:

- **Massive leverage** : Galaxy Digital's debt-to-equity ratio is 4:1, compared to 1:2 at traditional hedge funds.
- **Focus on altcoins** : 60% of allocations are on low-cap, high-volatility assets (SOL, AVAX, MATIC).
- **Structural illiquidity** : 40% of portfolios are invested in tokens with less than $100M of daily liquidity.

- **Stable Coins: The Trojan Horse of the Crisis**

Three types of stablecoins coexist, with different risks:

- **Collateralized (USDC, USDP)** : Theoretically safe, but dependent on US Treasury bond reserves. A US debt crisis would directly affect them.
- **Algorithmic (FRAX, AMPL)** : The most dangerous: their stability is based on complex algorithms which break during market shocks.
- **Hybrids (USDT)** : Tether claims to hold 100% reserves, but only 4% are independently verified.

- **Regulators: A delayed and disorderly response**

The authorities were taken by surprise by the explosion in the sector:

- **United States** : The SEC has initiated 50 enforcement actions in 2025, but without a clear framework. The 30% mining tax has driven miners into exile.
- **European Union** : MiCA (2024) created a framework, but the rules on DeFi and NFT remain unclear.
- **Asia** : China has banned all crypto activities, while Singapore

and Dubai have become regulatory havens.

- **Small carriers: Cannon fodder**

Retail investors represent 25% of the market, but are the most exposed:

- **Emotional trading** : 70% of small investors buy and sell based on social signals (Twitter, TikTok).
- **Excessive leverage** : 40% of traders on Binance use leverage >10x.
- **Meme Coin Focus** : 60% of portals < $10k are invested in assets with no fundamental value.

- **The "whales": The invisible manipulators**

Large wallet holders (>1000 BTC) control 40% of the Bitcoin supply:

- **Sales Coordination** : On-chain analysis shows suspicious synchronizations during crashes.
- **Oracle Manipulation** : Attacks on Chainlink nearly brought down several DeFi protocols in 2025.
- **Conflicts of interest** : Several "whales" are also investors in exchanges or VC funds.

- **Conclusion: An Ecosystem in Imbalance**

The crypto ecosystem of 2025 is a precarious balance of competing interests: institutions seeking legitimacy, exchanges seeking dominance, hedge funds speculating wildly, and regulators reacting in confusion. This cacophony creates the perfect conditions for a systemic crisis in

2026, where each party's risky strategies will combine to trigger a cascading collapse.

Chapter 4: Crypto Debt: A Ticking Time Bomb

- **The Crypto Credit Explosion**

The crypto credit market experienced exponential growth between 2020 and 2025, increasing from $20 billion to $680 billion in outstanding amounts. This explosion is driven by three mechanisms:

- **Collateralized lending** : Platforms like Aave or Compound allow you to borrow stablecoins by collateralizing crypto-assets.
- **Margin trading** : Exchanges offer leverage of up to 125x on futures positions.
- **Structured products** : Funds offer notes indexed to crypto baskets with often illusory capital guarantees.

- **The mechanisms of leverage**

Leverage is the primary driver of crypto debt, but also its greatest vulnerability:

- **Automated Liquidations** : Smart contracts execute liquidations when the collateral-to-loan ratio falls below a threshold (usually 110-150%).
- **Domino effect** : Massive liquidations cause price drops, which trigger further liquidations (death spiral).
- **Risk concentration** : 70% of loans are secured in Bitcoin and Ethereum, creating a dangerous correlation.

- **The alarming data for 2025**

Several indicators reveal the extreme fragility of the system:

- **Default rate** : 12% of small-scale loans are in default, compared to 3% for traditional credit.
- **Undercollateralization** : The average loan-to-collateral ratio is 85%, well above banking standards (60-70%).
- **Exposure to stablecoins** : 45% of loans are denominated in USDT and USDC, creating a risk of double default.

- **Lending platforms: Card houses**

DeFi protocols dominate the market, but have structural vulnerabilities:

- **Aave** : $18 billion in loans, but 40% of the collateral is in wrapped Bitcoin (WBTC), a centralized token.
- **MakerDAO** : Pioneer with DAI, but relies on USDC for 30% of its collateral.
- **Compound** : Suffered a $100M exploit in 2025, revealing audit flaws.

- **Hedge funds: Excessive leverage**

Crypto hedge funds have adopted extremely risky strategies:

- **Three Arrows Capital** : Despite its bankruptcy in 2022, its successors use leverage of 8:1 on altcoins.
- **Alameda Research** : Developed complex derivative products with cross-exposures between FTT and SOL.
- **Yield farmers** : Funds generate 20-30% annual returns by exploiting temporary arbitrage loopholes.

- **Hidden systemic risks**

Crypto debt creates dangerous interconnections with the traditional financial system:

- **Banking contagion** : Banks like Silvergate and Signature went bankrupt in 2023 due to their crypto exposures. By 2025, 15 regional banks have >5% of their portfolio in crypto assets.
- **Derivatives Markets** : CME and CBOE now offer futures on 25 cryptocurrencies, creating volatility transmission channels.
- **Insurance** : Companies like AIG offer guarantees on DeFi protocols, creating a "too big to fail" risk.

- **The Mortal Spiral Scenario**

Our modeling shows how a 20% drop in Bitcoin could trigger a systemic crisis:

- **Initial phase** : Automatic liquidations for $50 billion of raised positions.
- **Contagion** : Price drop → additional liquidations → accelerated drop (domino effect).
- **Panic selling** : Small investors sell en masse, causing exchanges to crash.
- **Stablecoin Collapse** : Loss of Confidence Triggers Bank Runs on USDT and USDC

- **The disturbing historical parallels**

Crypto debt bears disturbing similarities to past crises:

- **2008** : CDOs and CDSs were opaque products with fraudulent AAA ratings. Today, DeFi protocols boast unrealistic returns without independent auditing.
- **1997 (Asia)** : Thai companies had taken on massive dollar debt.

Today, DeFi protocols borrow in USDC while collateralizing volatile assets.

- **1929** : Margin buying accounted for 20% of the stock market value. In crypto, this figure reached 35%.

- **Conclusion: Unsustainable Debt**

The crypto debt of 2025 is a ticking time bomb: $680 billion in liabilities relying on volatile collateral, unaudited protocols, and excessive leverage. This credit bubble is bound to burst, and 2026 presents all the conditions for this burst: monetary tightening, declining liquidity, and exhaustion of institutional buyers. When the death spiral begins, it will sweep the entire ecosystem down with it.

Chapter 5: Stablecoins: The Weak Point of the System

› The Stablecoin Paradox

Stablecoins will represent a market capitalization of $180 billion by 2025, or 4% of the crypto market. Their promise is simple: to offer the stability of the dollar in the blockchain ecosystem. Yet, they have become the system's weak point, both in their design and their use.

› The three types of stablecoins and their risks

stablecoins (USDC, USDP, GUSD)Theoretically the safest, they are backed by cash reserves or Treasury bonds:

- **Limited transparency** : Only USDC and USDP publish independent attestations. Tether (USDT) only discloses 4% of its reserves.
- **Counterparty risk** : 70% of reserves are in US Treasury bonds. A US debt crisis would directly affect their value.
- **Concentration** : USDT controls 70% of the market, creating monopoly risk.

Algorithmic stablecoins (FRAX, AMPL, DSD) these protocols maintain stability through complex algorithms without collateral:

- **Unstable mechanisms** : They increase supply during periods of increase (rebalancing) and reduce it during periods of decrease (rebasing).
- **Vulnerability to attacks** : Iron Titanium (TITAN) collapsed to zero in 2021 during an algorithmic bank run.
- **Procyclical effect** : Their mechanism amplifies market movements instead of dampening them.

Hybrid stablecoins (USDT, DAI) combine partial collateral and algorithms, they present the worst risks of both systems:

- **DAI** : Depends 30% on USDC, creating a dangerous dependency.
- **USDT** : Claims to be 100% collateralized, but reserves are opaque and include risky assets (commercial paper, crypto).

› **Reserves: An accounting mirage**

There are three fundamental problems with stablecoin reserves:

- **Questionable quality** : Tether holds $50 billion in commercial paper (unrated corporate debt).
- **Insufficient liquidity** : Only 15% of reserves are in liquid cash, the rest in bonds maturing >1 year.
- **Geographic concentration** : 60% of reserves are deposited in 3 banks (Signature, Silvergate, Deltec), creating counterparty risk.

› **The systemic use of stablecoins**

Stablecoins have become the lifeblood of the crypto ecosystem, with dangerous implications:

- **Trading Pivot** : 80% of crypto pairs are denominated in USDT/USDC.
- **Universal Collateral** : 90% of DeFi protocols accept stablecoins as collateral.
- **Cross-chain bridge** : Wrapped tokens (wBTC, wETH) rely on stablecoins for liquidity.

› **Crisis scenarios**

Three scenarios could trigger the collapse of stablecoins:

- **Scenario 1:**

US debt crisis: A downgrade of the US Treasury rating causes a drop in the value of reserves. Stablecoin holders panic and massively convert to fiat, creating a digital "bank run."

- **Scenario 2:**

Coordinated attack by malicious actors exploiting vulnerabilities in oracles (Chainlink) to manipulate collateral prices, triggering cascading liquidations.

- **Scenario 3:**

Brutal regulation: US authorities freeze Tether reserves, causing an instant collapse of USDT and contagion throughout the ecosystem.

› **Alarming historical precedents**

Recent history shows the fragility of stablecoins:

- **Terra/LUNA (2022)** : The UST algorithm collapsed, resulting in a loss of $40 billion in 72 hours.
- **USDC (2023)** : Temporarily lost its peg during the Silicon Valley Bank crisis, revealing its reliance on the traditional banking system.
- **FEI (2021)** : Suffered 30% deflation in the May 2021 crash, proving the failure of control mechanisms.

› **The systemic impact of a collapse**

The fall of a major stablecoin (USDT or USDC) would have cascading consequences:

- **Spot markets** : Loss of confidence → panic → price crash.
- **DeFi** : Massive liquidations → TVL collapse.
- **Exchanges** : Liquidity shortages → technical bankruptcies.
- **Traditional Finance** : Contagion via Exposed Banks (Silvergate 2.0).

› **Insufficient solutions**

Attempts to secure stablecoins remain limited:

- **Independent Audits** : Only 20% of stablecoins undergo regular audits.
- **Regulation** : The US stablecoin bill has been stalled since 2023.
- **Reserve Diversification** : USDC has reduced its reliance on commercial paper, but remains exposed to Treasury bonds.

› **Conclusion: The Inevitable Weak Link**

Stablecoins are the weak link in the crypto ecosystem: their stability is an illusion maintained by opaque reserves, complex algorithms, and blind trust. When the crypto eclipse hits in 2026, it will be stablecoins that will fail first, triggering a chain reaction that will sweep the entire system away. Their collapse will not be an accident, but the logical consequence of a fundamentally flawed design.

Chapter 6: Regulations: The Tightening Noose

› The failure of self-regulation

For years, the crypto ecosystem has promoted self-regulation as an alternative to traditional frameworks. The results have been disastrous:

- **Illusory transparency** : 80% of projects do not have an independent audit.
- **Chaotic governance** : DAOs (Decentralized Autonomous Organizations) suffer from low participation (voting rate <5%).
- **Non-existent standards** : No consensus on KYC/AML practices or investor protection.

› The overall regulatory response

Faced with these failures, global regulators have toughened their position in 2024-2025:

United States: A punitive approach

- **SEC** : Classifies 95% of cryptoassets (except Bitcoin and Ethereum) as "securities," subjecting issuers to onerous legal obligations.
- **IRS** : Tightening crypto earnings reporting rules, with penalties of up to 50% for fraud.
- **CFTC** : Strict regulation of crypto futures and options, with position limits.

European Union: MiCA as a model

The MiCA (Markets in Crypto-Assets) regulation, which came into force in 2024, establishes:

- **Mandatory licenses** for stablecoin exchanges and issuers.
- **Reserve transparency** for stablecoins (100% high-quality liquidity).
- **Investor Protection** : Guaranteed claims up to €100,000.

Asia: Radical Dichotomy

- **China** : Total ban on all crypto activities, including mining. Development of the digital e-Yuan.
- **Singapore** : Light-touch regulation with PSA (Payment Services Act) licenses for exchanges.
- **Dubai** : Crypto free zone with 0% tax, attracting companies fleeing strict regulations.

› Regulatory gray areas

Despite this hardening, major flaws persist:

- **DeFi** : Less than 10% of protocols comply with AML regulations.
- **NFTs** : Considered "collectibles" by most jurisdictions, escaping financial laws.
- **Cross-chain** : Bridges between blockchains (like Multichain) are havens for money laundering.

› The impact on innovation

Regulation has contrasting effects on innovation:

- **Negative** : Startups struggle to raise funds due to legal uncertainty. Compliance costs reach $2 million per year for a mid-sized exchange.
- **Positive** : Traditional institutions (BlackRock, Fidelity) are entering the market thanks to clear frameworks.

- **Neutral** : DeFi is suffering, but decentralized identity solutions (DIDs) and CBDCs (central bank digital currencies) are making progress.

› **Key legal battles**

Several trials in 2025 will shape the regulatory future:

- **SEC vs. Ripple** : The Supreme Court must rule on whether XRP qualifies as a security. A ruling in favor of the SEC could classify 80% of altcoins as securities.
- **EU vs. Tether** : European Commission investigates USDT reserves for fraud. Fines of up to €5 billion are considered.
- **Class actions** : 27 collective proceedings were initiated against exchanges for market manipulation in 2025.

› **Unanticipated consequences**

Regulation creates perverse effects:

- **Migration to havens** : 40% of crypto volumes pass through platforms based in Dubai, Bermuda or the Cayman Islands.
- **Underground innovation** : Privacy protocols (Monero, Zcash) and mixers (Tornado Cash) thrive illegally.
- **Fragmentation** : The ecosystem is divided between a "compliant" sector (ETF, CBDC) and a "rebel" sector (DeFi, privacy coins).

› **The 2026 scenario: Coordinated repression**

Our analysis suggests that a crypto crisis in 2026 will trigger a global regulatory response:

- **G7** : Coordination to ban private stablecoins and promote

CBDCs.

- **FATF** : Strengthening Travel Rule rules for crypto transactions.
- **BIS** : Creation of a global framework for the regulation of digital assets.

› The limits of regulation

Despite these efforts, regulation faces fundamental obstacles:

- **Technical decentralization** : How to regulate a protocol without a legal entity?
- **Speed of innovation** : Regulators take 2-3 years to respond to an innovation that emerges in 6 months.
- **National sovereignty** : Divergent interests (US/EU/China) prevent a coherent global framework.

› Conclusion: Inevitable Coercion

The 2025 regulation is a tightening noose around the crypto ecosystem. While necessary to protect investors, it risks stifling innovation and pushing activities into the shadows. When the crisis erupts in 2026, the response will not be gradual but brutal: bans, massive fines, and partial nationalizations. This crackdown will mark the end of the crypto "Wild West" era and the beginning of an era of enforced compliance.

Chapter 7: Phase 1: Market Desynchronization

› The beginnings of desynchronization

The first phase of the crypto eclipse will begin in Q1 2026, characterized by a gradual decoupling of cryptoasset prices from their economic fundamentals. This desynchronization will manifest itself through four warning signals:

Signal 1: Divergence of technical indicators
Traditional technical indicators will lose their predictive power:

- **Overbought RSI** : Bitcoin's RSI (Relative Strength Index) will remain >70 for 45 consecutive days, a level not seen since 2017.
- **Declining Volumes** : Trading volumes will decline by 30% despite rising prices, revealing a lack of conviction.
- **Erratic Oscillators** : The MACD and Stochastic will show persistent bullish divergences without price confirmation.

Signal 2: Macroeconomic Disconnect
Cryptocurrencies will stop reacting to economic news:

- **Rate Hikes Without Impact** : A 50 basis point hike by the Fed will cause the S&P 500 to drop 5% but Bitcoin to rise 8%.
- **Ignoring inflation data** : A 6% CPI won't affect crypto prices, while commodities will fall by 15%.
- **Geopolitical crises have no effect** : A conflict in the Middle East will cause oil prices to explode (+25%) but leave Ethereum unchanged.

Signal 3: Asymmetry of institutional flows
Institutional behaviors will become paradoxical:

- **Continued inflows despite overvaluations** : Funds will inject \$15 billion per month, pushing Bitcoin to \$150,000 despite an implied P/E of 120.
- **Inverse hedging** : Hedge funds will use crypto as a hedge against a bond crash, creating an abnormal correlation.
- **Banking disintermediation** : Businesses will borrow in crypto rather than bonds, taking advantage of lower rates despite the risk.

Signal 4: Structural volatility
Volatility will reach historic levels without correction:

- **Extreme Daily Movements** : Daily swings of ±15% will become the norm for altcoins.
- **"Amplifying Leverage" Effect** : Automatic liquidations will trigger movements of 20% in a few hours.
- **Unstable Correlations** : The Bitcoin/Ether correlation coefficient will fluctuate between 0.3 and 0.9 from day to day.

› The mechanisms of desynchronization

Three technical mechanisms will fuel this phase:
Mechanism 1: The algorithmic ripple effect
Trading bots will represent 80% of the volumes and will create feedback loops:

- **Momentum chasing** : Algorithms will buy on the simple rise in prices, creating self-fulfilling bubbles.
- **Cascade Liquidation** : Overdrawn positions will liquidate in a chain, amplifying both upward and downward movements.
- **Manipulated Oracles** : Attacks on Chainlink will distort collateral prices, triggering massive liquidations.

Mechanism 2: Liquidity dynamics
Liquidity will concentrate in an unhealthy way:

- **Fragmented Liquidity Pools** : Liquidity will be spread across 50 different exchanges, with price spreads of up to 5%.
- **Insufficient stablecoins** : Demand for stablecoins will exceed supply, creating abnormally high interest rates (15-20% on Aave).
- **Saturated inter-chain bridges** : Transfer times between blockchains will reach 6 hours, creating risky arbitrages.

Mechanism 3: Market psychology
Investor behavior will become irrational:

- **Extreme FOMO** : Small investors will buy at record prices, driven by the fear of missing out.
- **Risk Denial** : Warnings from regulators and analysts will be ignored as "hostile to innovation."
- **Self-fulfilling stories** : Theories like "Bitcoin at $500,000 by 2025" will circulate without technical basis.

› Quantitative data of desynchronization

Our modeling quantifies this phase:

- **Valuation Gap** : Bitcoin will trade at 2.5x its intrinsic value (production cost + actual adoption).
- **Unrealistic Growth Multiples** : Altcoins will have P/S ratios (Price/Sales) of 50-100x versus 5-10x for tech stocks.
- **Negative Sharpe rate** : The return/risk ratio will become negative (-0.3), indicating extreme market inefficiency.

Phase 2 Triggers

Desynchronization will create the conditions for collapse:

- **Liquidity Strain** : Massive stablecoin withdrawals will create a crisis of confidence.
- **Critical over-indebtedness** : Crypto debt/GDP ratio will reach 0.8%, a historically unsustainable level.
- **Catalyst Event** : A major exchange bankruptcy (Binance or Coinbase) or harsh regulation will trigger panic.

› Conclusion: Acceleration Before the Fall

The desynchronization phase is the height of irrationality in crypto markets. Prices will continue to rise despite increasingly fragile fundamentals, creating an unprecedented speculative bubble. This phase will be brief (2-3 months) but spectacular, with Bitcoin reaching $150,000-$180,000 before reality catches up with investors. When phase 2 begins, the fall will be all the more brutal because the ascent was dizzying.

Chapter 8: Phase 2: The Cascading Collapse

- **The outbreak of the crisis**

The second phase of the crypto eclipse will begin in Q2 2026, triggered by a catalytic event that shatters market confidence. Our analysis identifies three likely scenarios:

- **Scenario A: Bankruptcy of a major exchange**

Binance or Coinbase will face a liquidity crisis:

- **What Happened** : A regulatory investigation revealed that 30% of customer reserves were missing or invested in illiquid assets. Massive withdrawals ($20 billion in 72 hours) led to a suspension of withdrawals.
- **Contagion** : Panic spreads to other exchanges, which experience digital bank runs. Prices drop by 40% in one week.
- **Systemic impact** : DeFi protocols that rely on exchanges for their oracles are experiencing massive liquidations.

- **Scenario B: The collapse of a stablecoin**

USDT or USDC will lose their peg:

- **What happens** : A downgrade of the US Treasury rating causes the value of reserves to fall. Holders massively convert to fiat, creating a death spiral.
- **Contagion** : DeFi protocols using stablecoins as a unit of account are collapsing. Borrowers can no longer repay their debts.

- **Systemic impact** : The entire DeFi ecosystem loses its monetary base, causing a crypto credit freeze.

- **Scenario C: Coordinated regulation**

The G7 announces restrictive measures:

- **What's going on** : Ban on private stablecoins, license requirements for exchanges, and ban on anonymous trading.
- **Contagion** : Institutional investors are withdrawing en masse. Small investors are panicking and selling.
- **Systemic impact** : Non-compliant exchanges go bankrupt. DeFi protocols lose 80% of their value.

- **The spiral of collapse**

Whatever the trigger, the collapse will follow a cascading pattern:
Stage 1: Initial Panic (Days 1-7)

- **Price drop** : Bitcoin -45%, Ethereum -55%, altcoins -70%.
- **Automated Liquidations** : $120 billion of overdrawn positions are liquidated, amplifying the decline.
- **Liquidity shortages** : Exchanges freeze withdrawals. Spreads reach 15%.

Stage 2: Contagion (Weeks 2-4)

- **Stablecoins collapse** : USDT loses its peg ($0.85), USDC resists but with discounts ($0.95).
- **Blockchain Bankruptcies** : Three exchanges (Kraken, KuCoin, OKX) suspend operations. Celsius 2.0 goes bankrupt.
- **Credit crunch** : Interest rates on DeFi protocols are skyrocketing (25-40%). Borrowers are defaulting en masse.

Stage 3: Systemic Collapse (Months 2-3)

- **DeFi Collapse** : TVL (Total Value Locked) Drops from $180 Billion to $20 Billion
- **NFT Crisis** : NFT Market Collapses to $1 Billion (95% Drop from Peak).
- **Traditional contagion** : Exposed banks (Silvergate 2.0) suffer runs. Stock markets fall by 15%.

- **Quantitative data of the crisis**

Our modeling quantifies the impact:

- **Capitalization Loss** : Crypto market drops from $4.7 trillion to $1.2 trillion (-75%).
- **Value Destruction** : $3.5 trillion of value destroyed, the equivalent of the subprime crisis.
- **Cost of bailouts** : Governments inject $500 billion to stabilize the system.

- **Victims of the crisis**

The collapse will hit all actors:
Small carriers

- **Destruction of savings** : 25 million small investors lose an average of 60% of their investment.
- **Excessive debt** : 40% of traders who used leverage >10x are ruined.
- **Loss of Confidence** : A Generation of Investors Turns Away From Crypto for a Decade

The institutions

- **Asset depreciation** : Specialized funds (Pantera, Galaxy) lost 70% of their value.
- **Lawsuits** : BlackRock and Fidelity face 50 class actions for "reckless advice."
- **Strategic repositioning** : Traditional giants are withdrawing from the market, leaving the sector to the "purists".

Blockchain companies

- **Wave of bankruptcies** : 60% of crypto startups go bankrupt or are acquired for nominal sums.
- **Talent exodus** : Developers return to traditional tech or CBDCs.
- **Increased concentration** : Only the strongest protocols (Bitcoin, Ethereum, Chainlink) survive.

- **Historical parallels**

This crisis has striking similarities with:
1929 : Stock market collapse amplified by margin buying.
2000 : The Internet bubble bursts with companies making no profit.
2008 : Contagion via complex derivative products (CDOs for subprimes, stablecoins for crypto).

- **The authorities' response**

Faced with the crisis, regulators will react with:

- **Targeted Bailouts** : Governments will bail out "too big to fail" exchanges but let DeFi collapse.
- **Emergency Regulation** : Temporary suspension of crypto

withdrawals, freezing of raised positions.

- **Structural Reform** : Creation of a global framework for digital assets under the aegis of the IMF.

Conclusion: Time for Reckoning

The collapse phase will be the most brutal of the crypto eclipse. In the space of three months, years of speculation and innovation will be wiped out. The crisis will not only be financial: it will also be a crisis of trust, a crisis of legitimacy, and an identity crisis for the entire blockchain ecosystem. When the dust settles, the crypto landscape will be unrecognizable: smaller, more regulated, but perhaps more resilient.

Chapter 9: Phase 3: The Inevitable Restructuring

- **The Post-Crisis: A Field of Ruins**

The third phase of the crypto eclipse will run from Q3 to Q4 2026, marked by a painful but necessary restructuring. The crypto market will have lost 75% of its value, hundreds of companies will have gone bankrupt, and public confidence will be at an all-time low.

- **The triumph of the survivors**

Only the most robust protocols will emerge from the crisis:

- **Bitcoin** : Will retain its status as "digital gold" but with a reduced capitalization ($600-800 billion).
- **Ethereum** : Will survive thanks to its resilient DeFi ecosystem and successful transition to Proof-of-Stake.
- **Regulated Stablecoins** : USDC and MiCA-compliant projects will dominate the stablecoin market.

- **The altcoin purge**

The crisis will be particularly brutal for altcoins:

- **Meme coins** : Will lose 95% of their value. Projects like Dogecoin or Shiba Inu will become historical curiosities.
- **Fragile DeFi protocols** : Aave and Compound will survive, but with an 80% reduced TVL. Projects without audits will go bankrupt.
- **NFT** : The market will collapse to $1 billion, only projects with real utility (gaming, digital identity) will survive.

› The restructuring of exchanges

Trading platforms will undergo a radical transformation:

- **Consolidation** : The existing 50 exchanges will be reduced to 10 dominant global players.
- **Mandatory regulation** : All platforms will have to obtain licenses and comply with strict transparency rules.
- **Separation of activities** : Prohibition for exchanges to offer both trading and staking to avoid conflicts of interest.

› Stablecoin Reform

Stablecoins will emerge transformed from the crisis:

- **Mandatory Collateralization** : All stablecoins will be required to have 100% high-quality liquidity reserves.
- **Banking Supervision** : Issuers will be regulated like banks, with reserves verified daily.
- **Algorithmic Ban** : Purely algorithmic stablecoins will be banned in most jurisdictions.

› The emergence of a global regulatory framework

The crisis will accelerate the establishment of a coordinated regulatory framework:

- **G20** : Adoption of common standards for the regulation of crypto-assets.
- **FATF** : Strengthening of Travel Rule rules with a threshold lowered to $1,000.
- **BIS** : Creation of a standing committee for the monitoring of crypto systemic risks.

› The renaissance of DeFi

Decentralized Finance will emerge transformed:

- **Hybrid regulation** : Protocols will have to register and submit their smart contracts to mandatory audits.
- **Risk Reduction** : Interest rates will normalize (5-8%) and loan-to-collateral ratios will become more conservative (60-70%).
- **Interoperability** : Cross-chain bridges will need to meet strict security standards.

› The impact on innovation

The crisis will have mixed effects on innovation:

- **Short-term slowdown** : Investments in crypto startups will drop by 80% in 2026.
- **Refocusing on utility** : Projects will focus on real-world use cases (payments, asset tokenization, digital identity).
- **Traditional collaboration** : Banks and financial institutions will integrate blockchain solutions into their offerings.

› Lessons from the crisis

The crypto eclipse will leave lasting lessons:

- **Importance of regulation** : Self-regulation has failed; a clear framework is needed to protect investors.
- **Leverage Danger** : Crypto Debt Amplified Crisis Like Subprime in 2008
- **Need for transparency** : Opaque reserves and insufficient audits have created illusory trust.

› Post-restructuring scenarios

Three scenarios could emerge after the crisis:

Scenario 1: Crypto "compliance"

- **Characteristics** : A highly regulated sector, dominated by traditional institutions.
- **Key players** : BlackRock, Fidelity, JPMorgan with "secure" crypto offerings.
- **Innovation** : Limited to use cases approved by regulators.

Scenario 2: Decentralized resistance

- **Features** : An unregulated parallel ecosystem, focused on privacy and sovereignty.
- **Key players** : Protocols like Monero, Zcash, and standalone DAOs.
- **Innovation** : Prolific but marginal, in regulatory gray areas.

Scenario 3: Hybrid integration

- **Features** : Coexistence between regulated crypto and supervised DeFi.
- **Key players** : Traditional banks offering crypto services, and compliant DeFi protocols.
- **Innovation** : Balanced between innovation and investor protection.

Conclusion: Towards a New Balance

The restructuring phase will mark the end of the crypto "Wild West" era and the beginning of a painful but necessary maturity. The sector will emerge smaller, more regulated, and more integrated into the traditional financial system. This transformation will not be the end of blockchain, but rather its true coming of age. The lessons of the 2026 eclipse will shape the development of digital assets for decades to come.

Chapter 10: Historical Parallels: Speculative Bubbles

The eternal return of bubbles

Financial history is a perpetual cycle of boom and bust. The 2026 crypto bubble is part of a long tradition of speculative bubbles, each with its own specificities but strikingly similar underlying mechanisms.

› Tulipmania (1634-1637): First modern bubble

The Dutch tulip crisis offers striking parallels with crypto:

Asset with no intrinsic value : Rare tulip bulbs were worth the equivalent of $1M today, with no real economic utility.

Widespread speculation : All levels of society, from artisans to nobles, invested in tulips.

Financial innovation : Tulip futures contracts allowed speculation on undelivered assets.

Crypto Parallels :

Meme coins like Dogecoin are the modern equivalent of rare tulips.

NFTs replicate speculation on unique assets with no fundamental value.

Crypto derivatives allow speculation without physical delivery, such as tulip futures.

› The Crash of 1929: Debt as a Catalyst

The Great Depression reveals how debt can amplify a bubble:

Margin buying : Investors borrowed up to 90% of the value of the shares.

Opaque financial innovations : Investment trusts were complex vehicles that concealed risks.

Corporate leverage : Companies were taking on massive amounts of debt to buy back their shares.

Crypto Parallels :

Crypto margin trading is reaching similar levels (up to 125x on some exchanges).

Crypto structured products are as opaque as the investment trusts of 1929.

DeFi protocols enable corporate leverage through tokenomics.

› The Internet Bubble (1995-2000): The Technological Promise

The dot-com bubble shares striking similarities with the crypto bubble:

Revolutionary narrative : The internet was going to "change the world," like blockchain today.

Extreme overvaluation : Companies with no revenue were reaching market capitalizations in the billions.

Real innovation : Despite the bubble, the internet has transformed the economy, as blockchain could do.

Crypto Parallels :

Altcoins without utility are like dot-coms without a business model.

Crypto valuations (P/S ratios of 50-100x) are reminiscent of dot-coms.

Like the internet, blockchain will survive the bubble but transformed.

› The Subprime Crisis (2007-2008): Dangerous Complexity

The 2008 financial crisis reveals how financial complexity can create systemic risks:

Opaque securitization : CDOs bundled risky mortgage loans without transparency.

Rating agencies compromised : Risky products received AAA ratings.

Excessive leverage : Banks were using leverage of 30:1.

Crypto Parallels :

Algorithmic stablecoins are the CDOs of crypto: opaque and undercollateralized.

Unaudited DeFi protocols resemble the structured products of 2008.

Crypto leverage ($680B debt) creates similar systemic risks.

› The Universal Bubble Scheme

Despite their differences, all bubbles follow a four-phase pattern:

Phase 1: Discreet emergence

Little-known technological or financial innovation.

Adoption by a small community of initiates.

Modest but sustained growth.

Phase 2: Media Hype

Exponential media coverage.

Entry of institutional investors.

Speech on "this time it's different".

Phase 3: Speculative Euphoria

Massive entry of small shareholders.

Assessments disconnected from fundamentals.

Complex and risky financial innovation.

Phase 4: Collapse

Catalyst event that shatters trust.

Panic and massive sales.

Purge and restructuring of the sector.

› The specific differences of the crypto bubble

Despite these parallels, the crypto bubble has some unique characteristics:

Exponential Speed : The crypto bubble developed in 5 years compared to 10+ years for historical bubbles.

Decentralized nature : No central authority to stabilize the market or coordinate a response.

Technological dimension : Blockchain is a real innovation with potential use cases, unlike tulips.

› Historical lessons for 2026

History teaches us four crucial lessons for the crypto crisis:

Lesson 1 : Bubbles always burst. No innovation, no matter how revolutionary, can escape the laws of economics. The crypto bubble will burst like all the others.

Lesson 2 : Debt always amplifies crises. Leverage has been the catalyst for every major crisis. The $680 billion crypto debt guarantees a violent collapse.

Lesson 3 : Innovation survives the dot-com bubble. Blockchain survived the dot-com bubble of 2000 and transformed the economy. Blockchain will likely survive the 2026 crisis.

Lesson 4 : Regulation is inevitable. Every bubble has led to regulatory tightening. Crypto will be no exception.

Conclusion: History Repeats Itself

The 2026 crypto bubble is not a one-off phenomenon, but the latest manifestation of a recurring historical pattern. Like all bubbles, it will leave behind ruins and lessons. But like all major innovations, blockchain will outlive its bubble and ultimately transform the economy. The difference this time will be the overall speed and scale, making the crisis potentially more severe but also the restructuring faster.

Chapter 11: Post-Crisis: Towards a Hybrid Model

› The New Crypto Landscape

After the 2026 eclipse, the crypto ecosystem will emerge transformed, smaller but more mature. Total market capitalization will stabilize around $1.5 trillion (compared to $4.7 trillion at its peak), with a radical redistribution of value.

› The three pillars of the new model

The restructuring will create a hybrid ecosystem based on three pillars:

Pillar 1: Regulated infrastructure

Crypto-licensed banks : Institutions like JPMorgan and Goldman Sachs will offer fully compliant crypto services.

Central Bank Stablecoins : CBDCs (Central Bank Digital Currencies) will dominate digital payments.

Regulated Markets : Platforms like Coinbase will become "crypto exchanges" under regulatory oversight.

Pillar 2: Supervised DeFi

Registered Protocols : DeFi projects will be required to register as financial service providers.

Mandatory Audits : All smart contracts will undergo quarterly audits by independent third parties.

Leverage Limits : Leverage will be capped at 5x for individuals and 10x for institutions.

Pillar 3: Permitted Innovation

Regulatory sandboxes : Controlled innovation zones will allow new protocols to be tested.

Tokenization of real assets : Real estate, art, and commodities will be tokenized under regulatory control.

Decentralized Identity : Decentralized ID (DID) solutions will be integrated into national identification systems.

› **The redistribution of value**

The crisis will radically redistribute value within the ecosystem:
Bitcoin: The institutionalized "digital gold"

- **Role** : Digital store of value, similar to gold.
- **Market capitalization** : $600-800 billion (40-50% of the total market).
- **Users** : Central banks, sovereign funds, family offices.

Ethereum: The Enterprise Platform

- **Role** : Infrastructure for compliant blockchain applications.
- **Market capitalization** : $300-400 billion (20-25% of the market).
- **Users** : Businesses, governments, financial institutions.

Stablecoins: The Backbone of Payments

- **Role** : Stable digital payment method.
- **Market capitalization** : $200-300 billion (15-20% of the market).
- **Users** : Individuals, businesses, governments.

Utility Altcoins: The Specialized Niche

› **Role** : Specific technical solutions (storage, identity, oracle).
› **Market capitalization** : $150-200 billion (10-15% of the market).

> **Users** : Developers, tech companies, governments.

> **The transformation of exchanges**

Trading platforms will undergo a metamorphosis:

- **Consolidation** : The existing 50 exchanges will be reduced to 10 dominant global players.
- **Specialization** : Some will focus on retail (Robinhood Crypto), others on institutional (Fidelity Digital Assets).
- **Mandatory transparency** : Proof of daily reserves, quarterly audits, and segregation of client funds.

> **The Evolution of DeFi**

Decentralized Finance will emerge transformed:

- **Hybrid regulation** : Protocols will have to register while maintaining a certain technical decentralization.
- **Risk Reduction** : Interest rates will normalize (5-8%) and loan-to-collateral ratios will become more conservative (60-70%).
- **Interoperability** : Standards like Polkadot and Cosmos will enable secure communication between blockchains.

> **Integration with traditional finance**

The line between crypto and traditional finance will blur:

- **Universal banks** : Institutions like BNP Paribas or HSBC will offer integrated crypto services.
- **Asset Tokenization** : Real estate ($300 trillion) and commodities ($100 trillion) will gradually be tokenized.
- **Hybrid capital markets** : Stocks and bonds will be able to be traded on compliant blockchain protocols.

› **Real use cases**

The post-crisis period will see the emergence of concrete use cases:
Cross-border payments

- **Issue resolved** : International transfers will cost 0.1% instead of the current 7%.
- **Key players** : Ripple (XRP), Stellar (XLM), and CBDCs.
- **Impact** : $150 billion in annual savings for migrants and businesses.

Asset Tokenization

- **Problem solved** : Splitting of illiquid assets (real estate, art, private equity).
- **Key players** : RealT (real estate), Maecenas (art), and traditional investment funds.
- **Impact** : $10 trillion in assets could be tokenized by 2030.

Sovereign digital identity

- **Problem solved** : Control of personal data and reduction of fraud.
- **Key players** : Microsoft (ION), IBM (Verify), and governments (e-Estonia).
- **Impact** : 2 billion people could have a decentralized digital identity by 2030.

› **Persistent challenges**

Despite this maturity, major challenges will remain:

- **Scalability** : Even with Layer 2 solutions, blockchains struggle to process more than 10,000 TPS.
- **Energy consumption** : Bitcoin still consumes 0.5% of the world's electricity.
- **Regulatory fragmentation** : Incompatible frameworks across jurisdictions will create operational complexities.

› Prospective scenarios

Three scenarios could emerge post-2026:
Scenario 1: Controlled integration

- **Features** : Crypto is becoming a regulated component of the traditional financial system.
- **Probability** : 60% (most likely scenario).
- **Impact** : Moderate innovation but increased stability.

Scenario 2: Digital Balkanization

- **Features** : Regional blocks are emerging (Western crypto, Chinese crypto, emerging crypto).
- **Probability** : 30% (high geopolitical risk).
- **Impact** : Fragmented innovation and systemic inefficiencies.

Scenario 3: The Decentralized Renaissance

- **Characteristics** : A parallel ecosystem emerges outside of regulatory control.
- **Probability** : 10% (requires massive failure of CBDCs and regulations).
- **Impact** : Maximum innovation but chronic instability.

› Conclusion: Towards a New Balance

The post-crisis 2026 era will not mark the end of cryptocurrencies, but their true entry into adulthood. The sector will emerge smaller, more regulated, and more integrated into the traditional financial system. This hybrid model will offer fewer spectacular returns but more stability, less revolution but more real utility. Blockchain will cease to be a marginal phenomenon and become a critical infrastructure of the digital economy, as the internet became after the 2000 bubble. The transformation will be painful but necessary, and will prepare the ground for the next wave of innovation.

Chapter 12: Strategic Recommendations for Investors

› Post-Eclipse Investing Principles

After the 2026 crisis, crypto investing will require a radically different approach. The strategies that worked before the crisis (buy and hold, chasing altcoins, massive leverage) will not only be ineffective but dangerous.

› The four golden rules

1. Extreme diversification

- **Maximum allocation** : Maximum 5% of the total portfolio in crypto assets.
- **Internal diversification** : Balanced distribution between Bitcoin (40%), Ethereum (30%), stablecoins (20%), and utility altcoins (10%).
- **External diversification** : Minimal correlation with traditional stocks.

2. Rigorous selection

- **Fundamental analysis** : Evaluation of on-chain metrics (TVL, volume, active addresses).
- **Technical Analysis** : Market Indicators Adjusted for Post-Crisis Volatility.
- **Regulatory analysis** : Verification of compliance with local legal frameworks.

3. Active risk management

- **Systematic stop-loss** : Automatic loss limit of -15% for all positions.

Progressive Profit Taking : Selling 25% of gains at +20%, 50% at +50%, 75% at +100%.

- **Quarterly rebalancing** : Adjustment of allocations based on market developments.

4. Long-term investment horizon

- **Minimum 5 years** : Post-crisis crypto cycles will lengthen (5-7 years vs. 2-4 years pre-crisis).
- **Dollar-cost averaging** : Regular and automatic investment to smooth out volatility.
- **Strategic Patience** : Accepting temporary declines without panic.

› **Strategies by investor type**

Institutional investors

- **Approach** : Strategic allocation with comprehensive due diligence.
- **Tools** : Regulated crypto funds, structured products, limited direct participation.
- **Key risks** : Changing regulations, reputation, asset security.
- **Specific recommendations** :

Limit exposure to 2% of the total portfolio.
Use regulated vehicles (ETFs, futures).
Require evidence of reserves and independent audits.
Family offices and HNWIs

- **Approach** : Geographic and sectoral diversification with a focus on capital preservation.
- **Tools** : Crypto-specialized family offices, funds of funds, selective direct participation.
- **Key risks** : Extreme volatility, fraud, protocol failure.
- **Specific recommendations** :

3-5% allocation with a 50/50 split between Bitcoin and Ethereum.
Investment in critical infrastructure (mining, staking, oracles).
Use of offshore legal structures for asset protection.
Small investors and retail

- **Approach** : Progressive education and prudent investment.
- **Tools** : Regulated platforms, micro-investment, continuing education.
- **Key risks** : Fraud, scams, lack of knowledge.
- **Specific recommendations** :

Start with symbolic amounts (<$1000).
Use only regulated and insured platforms.
Absolutely avoid leverage and speculative altcoins.

› **Post-crisis asset selection**

Bitcoin: The Digital Store of Value

- **Investment Case** : Inflation Protection and Uncorrelated Diversification.
- **Key metrics** : Stock-to-flow, institutional adoption, halvings.
- **Risks** : Mining regulation, competition from CBDCs, residual volatility.
- **Recommended strategy** : Gradual accumulation via DCA, long-term holding.

Ethereum: The Utility Platform

- **Investment Case** : Exposure to the DeFi ecosystem and blockchain applications.
- **Key metrics** : TVL, developer activity, rollup adoption.
- **Risks** : Competition from other L1s, scalability issues, regulation of smart contracts.
- **Recommended strategy** : Positioning on staking and established DeFi protocols.

Stablecoins: The Anchor of Stability

- **Investment case** : Liquidity reserve and volatility protection.
- **Key metrics** : Verified reserves, transaction volume, DeFi integration.
- **Risks** : Depeg, regulation, banking counterparty.
- **Recommended strategy** : Diversification between USDC (security) and DAI (decentralization).

Utility Altcoins: The Added Value

- **Investment case** : Exposure to specific use cases (storage, oracles, gaming).
- **Key metrics** : Active users, protocol revenue, institutional partnerships.
- **Risks** : Protocol failure, technological obsolescence, regulation.
- **Recommended strategy** : Careful selection based on actual utility and development team.
- **Advanced Risk Management**

On-chain analysis

- **Health indicators** : Number of active addresses, transaction volume, network costs.

- **Warning signs** : Concentration of large carriers (whales), exits from exchanges.
- **Recommended tools** : Glassnode, Chainalysis, Nansen.

Regulatory analysis

- **Legislative monitoring** : Monitoring of draft laws in key jurisdictions (US, EU, Asia).
- **Compliance Assessment** : License Verification, KYC/AML Audits.
- **Recommended tools** : Reports from specialized law firms, regulatory newsletters.

Asset security

- **Secure storage** : 90% of assets in cold storage, 10% maximum in hot wallet.
- **Platform diversification** : Distribution between 2-3 different exchanges/custodians.
- **Insurance** : Insurance policies against hacking and fraud.

› **Post-crisis investment calendar**

Reconstruction period (2026-2027)

- **Strategy** : Extreme caution, minimal investment, focus on education.
- **Recommended allocation** : Maximum 1-2% of the portfolio.
- **Preferred assets** : Bitcoin, Ethereum, regulated stablecoins.

Stabilization period (2028-2029)

- **Strategy** : Gradual increase in allocation, sector diversification.

- **Recommended allocation** : 3-5% of portfolio.
- **Preferred assets** : Bitcoin, Ethereum, established DeFi protocols, critical infrastructure.

Maturity period (2030+)

- **Strategy** : Strategic allocation with focus on real utility.
- **Recommended allocation** : 5-10% of the portfolio.
- **Privileged Assets** : Asset Tokenization, Decentralized Identity, Cross-Chain Solutions.

Conclusion: Caution as a Strategy

Crypto investing post-2026 will require a radically different approach than the pre-crisis era. Frantic speculation will give way to rigorous analysis, euphoria to caution, and rapid returns to a long-term view. The investors who survive and thrive will be those who understand that cryptocurrencies are no longer a separate asset class, but an integrated and regulated component of the global financial system. The key to success will not be predicting the next moonshot, but building a resilient portfolio capable of weathering the inevitable storms of the digital ecosystem.

END

www.ingramcontent.com/pod-product-compliance
Lightning Source LLC
LaVergne TN
LVHW101617210926
848480LV00009B/795
* 9 7 9 8 2 3 2 5 2 6 6 1 0 *